The Story of My Life in Christ

A GUIDED DEVOTIONAL JOURNAL

MERLIN & THERESA BUHL

BILL CROWDER, GENERAL EDITOR

Our Daily Bread
Publishing™

The first version of this book, titled *My Hope to You: A Month-Long Devotional Journey to Share Your Faith* was written by Greg Smith, under contract for My Hope to You, a ministry of the Joshua Outreach Group, Inc.

Requests for permission to quote from this book should be directed to:
Permissions Department, Our Daily Bread Publishing, PO Box 3566, Grand Rapids, MI 49501, or contact us by email at permissionsdept@odb.org.

Scripture quotations are taken from the Holy Bible, New International Version®, NIV®. Copyright © 1973, 1978, 1984, 2011 by Biblica, Inc.™ Used by permission of Zondervan. All rights reserved worldwide. www.zondervan.com.

Interior design by Michael J. Williams

ISBN: 978-1-64070-110-6

Library of Congress Cataloging-in-Publication Data Available

Printed in China
21 22 23 24 25 26 27 28 / 8 7 6 5 4 3 2 1

INTRODUCTION

As soon as I turned the key in the ignition, the speakers erupted to life with the thunderous noise of a rap "song." (I know, I'm showing my age.) As I struggled to find the volume knob, I heard the F-word being used more than by a sailor who'd smashed his thumb with hammer. While I am used to being "in the world" and am not easily shocked by bad language, what horrified me was that this was my 16-year-old son's car. My heart sank into the pit of my stomach. This was what my son was choosing to listen to. And he had just returned from an afternoon baseball game with his friends in the car. As a father, I was a heartbroken.

Fortunately, in my counseling training, I was taught never to show shock at what is being shared. In our role as parents to nine kids, this has been immensely helpful! So, while I was driving his car to the repair shop, I calmly reached out to my son and asked if we could have a chat when he got home that night. He immediately apologized for the music and agreed to talk later that evening.

He came home about 10:30 and explained to me that he and his friends used that music to get pumped up for games. I asked him what kind of witness he thought this was to his friends, some of whom are not believers. His response? "Dad, to be honest, I am not sure I even believe in God anymore."

My heart leapt. My pulse quickened. My mind raced. This was . . . *awesome!* He trusted me enough to be honest with me.

All of the sudden the music choice was a complete nonissue. It was merely a symptom. My son's heart was being assaulted by the Evil One through doubts. Our lives were about to intersect in a powerful, God-ordained way.

In that moment, I was able to share with him a part of my faith story. In college and beyond, I had struggled with those same doubts and questions, so I was able to emotionally and intellectually take a seat beside him. We looked at this question and others from a shared perspective as we talked into the night about eternal matters. He found a safe place with me and, more importantly, with God—a safe space to ask his questions and express his doubts. My son was on a journey to find his own path to God and I was invited to intersect with my God story. A father's broken heart turned into a father's thankful heart.

How about you? Do you have people in your life that need the grace, mercy, and love of the Father? Your kids? Your grandkids? Spouse? Friends? Employees? Do they need a safe place to be honest? Do you want to be that safe place?

Your God story is to be celebrated because it is amazing.

We all have a unique path to faith in Christ. Some came to Christ at an early age. Some get preoccupied with material or vocational pursuits. Some run down roads of self-absorption and debauchery before embracing the saving grace of God. Some are just pretty good people until God helps them realize being good isn't enough. Regardless of the path, once we come to faith in Christ, the end result is the same. Because of what Jesus did, we are saved from our sins and are awarded eternal life with Him. This is a drastically different outcome than that of the unbeliever. It's amazing because your story is the only one of its kind. It's amazing because you get to experience joy in His presence, forever. It's amazing because God wants to use your unique God story to touch others with His Story.

You might suppose that others, especially young people in your life, are not watching you or do not care what you think. Think again. In a recent survey conducted by My Hope to You (see video at MH2U.org), 98 percent of people ages of 13 to 29 stated they would find the faith story of their parents and grandparents very interesting and valuable. What's more, 100 percent said that they would read it! Is God calling you to intersect their story with your story in a real, personal connection?

Their story is to be intersected with your story because God wants them to experience His Story.

You are a living story being written by the very hand of God. Your life is part of God's Story. Every person you come into contact with is a person God loves and is pursuing. Whether you share a gentle word, a kind act, a gift, a word of encouragement, or your complete faith story, each connection is used by God to intersect people's stories with His Story. If you truly believe the hope that lies within you and grasp its significance, the love of God will shine through the story of your life in Christ.

And the Bible commands us to be ready:

> Always be prepared to give an answer to everyone who asks you to give the reason for the hope that you have. But do this with gentleness and respect. (1 Peter 3:15)

Story is one of the most powerful tools we have to communicate with each other. We all have one, and each is unique and valuable. And there's none more powerful than the story of your life in Christ. This devotional journal was created to assist you in capturing your story so that 1 Peter 3:15 becomes a reality in your life, and those you love can also experience your story!

We have written this journal in a 28-day format that works like a devotional workbook. We want you to have an experience that will help you engage the Scriptures as you seek to communicate God's redemptive and healing work in your life. As we've worked with others to tell their story, we realized that daily bite-size chunks will help you to more easily complete this seemingly monumental task. Taking the time to experience this 28-day journey will prepare you to recognize and accept God's next invitation to intersect another's faith path.

Unpacking your story in 28 days is not meant to be a burden. If you miss a day, give yourself grace. It's OK if it takes a bit longer, just don't skip a day.

Blessings to you as you prepare to share your own story of God's amazing grace!

—Merlin Buhl

HOW TO USE THIS BOOK

This is a four-week devotional journey providing a structured plan to help you prepare to share your faith with those you care about. The daily readings and activities follow a pattern that will help you write parts of your story each week. It's important to follow the system in sequence to build the content you will share, regardless of the way in which you will eventually share it.

	Sun. Focus	Mon. Focus	Tues. Focus	Wed. Focus	Thur. Focus	Fri. Focus	Sat. Focus
Week 1 How?	Worship	Reflect	Record	Record	Record	Read	Retreat and Write
Week 2 Why?	Worship	Reflect	Record	Record	Record	Read	Retreat and Write
Week 3 What?	Worship	Reflect	Record	Record	Record	Read	Retreat and Write
Week 4 Who?	Worship	Reflect	Record	Record	Record	Read	Retreat and Write

Each week has a theme, based around a question:

Week 1: *How* did you come to faith? Telling your faith story

Week 2: *Why* did you come to faith? Explaining the reasons you believe in Christ

Week 3: *What* do you believe? Turning the basis of your faith in Christ into a statement of faith

Week 4: *Who* do you care about? Identifying the person(s) with whom you want to share your faith

Each of the four weeks follows a daily rhythm:

Sunday: Worship

Monday: Reflect

Tuesday: Record

Wednesday: Record

Thursday: Record

Friday: Read

Saturday: Retreat and Write

Each day is numbered from 1 to 28 and follows a specific structure:

Theme

Focus

Scripture

Devotional Thoughts

Prayer

Activity

When you write, you'll want to follow some general guidelines:

Keep it clear and simple. Try to avoid "Christianese" that others might not understand.

Keep it real and honest. But don't disparage others in telling your story. You'll communicate God's grace by example!

Keep it focused and brief. You're more likely to follow through if you don't try to be too detailed; and the person you're sharing with will be more likely to hear what you have say if you keep it succinct.

HOW?
TELLING YOUR STORY

DAY 1 • SUNDAY

THEME: Begin at the Beginning

FOCUS: Worship. Rest and trust in the Lord.

Colossians 1:15–20

> The Son is the image of the invisible God, the firstborn over all creation. For in him all things were created: things in heaven and on earth, visible and invisible, whether thrones or powers or rulers or authorities; all things have been created through him and for him. He is before all things, and in him all things hold together. And he is the head of the body, the church; he is the beginning and the firstborn from among the dead, so that in everything he might have the supremacy. For God was pleased to have all his fullness dwell in him, and through him to reconcile to himself all things, whether things on earth or things in heaven, by making peace through his blood, shed on the cross.

Devotional Thoughts

Every journey, every project, begins at the beginning.

Over the next month, you're going on a journey to explain and share your faith. Along the way, you'll reflect deeply on what you believe and why, and how you came to believe it. You will almost certainly discover some things about your faith and yourself. This journey will be challenging. But if you persist, your efforts and your faithfulness will prove to be a worthwhile investment. And you will be better positioned to share your relationship with the Father with others.

The first thing to understand is that this devotional journey doesn't begin with you. Your story doesn't begin with you. Your story begins at The Beginning.

Read and reflect on today's Scripture, Colossians 1:15–20. Your story begins at the beginning of all things: The Son of God, Jesus Christ. In that passage, the original word that is translated "all things" means, literally, everything. Jesus Christ is the beginning of everything, including your story. He is the Author and the first word on the first page of your story, and all of the stories that have ever been—or ever will be—told or lived out.

But as you trust Him and follow Him, you can become grounded in the foundation of all things. Whatever happens during this month, and whatever happens when you share the story you create, know that Christ is King, that He is in control of all things. So, roll up your sleeves, get on your knees, open your Bible, and sharpen your pencil. Give this process to Him who is the beginning and Lord of everything. Rest in His love and care.

> *Lord, let me begin this journey with you, for you are the beginning of my story. Let my heart and mind be grounded in the truth of your lordship of all things. And, grounded in that truth, let me not be afraid to tell my story, for you are ultimately in control of all things, including my need of you. Amen.*

ACTIVITY: Worship

Go to church! Yes, times of private devotion and worship are an important part of the life of faith, but following Christ is not a private religion: Jesus calls us to community. In fact, the English word *church* comes from the Greek word for an assembly of citizens called out for a public meeting. We are those that have been called out by Christ to receive His rescue, to gratefully worship Him, and to faithfully serve Him. Remember, the purpose of *The Story of My Life in Christ* is for you to prepare to share your faith with others. So, as you prepare to do that, worship with others today and participate in the fellowship of your brothers and sisters in Christ.

Yes, they are imperfect, just like you, and just like the people you want to share with. All the better then to begin this journey by seeing what Christ can do for broken people like us.

HOW?
TELLING YOUR STORY

DAY 2 • MONDAY

THEME: The Author of Your Story

FOCUS: Reflect. Look back on how you got here.

1 John 4:13–16

> This is how we know that we live in him and he in us: He has given us his Spirit. And we have seen and testify that the Father has sent his Son to be the Savior of the world. If anyone acknowledges that Jesus is the Son of God, God lives in them and they in God. And so we know and rely on the love God has for us.

Devotional Thoughts

This month, you'll learn to share how you came to faith—your personal story. But before we focus on the details of your story, let's ask a more general question. How did we become His followers?

As our Scripture teaches us today, the Holy Spirit lives within us, affirming that we are in relationship with Him. The Father has sent His Son to be the Savior of the world, and the Holy Spirit initially opens our eyes and hearts to our need of Jesus. Then, the Holy Spirit gives us assurance that we live in Him and He in us. All of this reminds us that we love Him because He first loved us.

Even before coming to Christ, we are His creation, His handiwork. Psalm 139:13 expresses this most intimate and ultimate truth about ourselves: "For you created my inmost being; you knit me together in my mother's womb." If it helps you to think of it this way, He is the author and we are among the characters in the great story He is telling.

As John assures us, if you acknowledge that Jesus is the Son of God, God lives in you and you live in God. But *acknowledge* means more than just intellectually recognizing the fact that Jesus is God's Son. It means that our faith, hope, and confidence are in Him—not ourselves.

This idea is foundational to the life of faith. The last sentence of our Scripture today tells us that we must know and rely on God's love for us. That's faith, the faith you're going to explore and share on this devotional journey. And, we can trust that the Holy Spirit will help you to do just that.

Lord, help my faith be more than mere knowledge or simple belief that you exist. Let me genuinely acknowledge you as the Creator of this world and the Lord of my life. Help me to love you with all of my heart, mind, soul, and strength. Help me to put this truth on display in my words, my actions, and my relationships. Amen.

ACTIVITY: Reflect

Today, reflect on how you came to have faith in Christ. It didn't just "happen." Some sequence of events in your life led you to believe and to become a disciple of Jesus Christ. It might have happened in childhood, adulthood, or somewhere in between. It might have been fairly straightforward, or a long and winding road. Today, take time to recall that sequence. As you reflect on how you got here, jot down some simple notes. They'll be helpful for your journaling exercises this week.

HOW?
TELLING YOUR STORY

DAY 3 • TUESDAY

THEME: Many Paths to One Door

FOCUS: Record. List the sequence of events that brought you here.

John 14:6–7

> Jesus answered, "I am the way and the truth and the life. No one comes to the Father except through me. If you really know me, you will know my Father as well. From now on, you do know him and have seen him."

Devotional Thoughts

Today, we read Jesus's words from John 14. While all of us have our own stories and our own journeys, we nevertheless arrive at the same place—Jesus.

This teaching from our Lord came on the night before He went to the cross. His disciples were clearly troubled by His statements that He was leaving (see John 14:1–3), and, as a result they begin to pepper Him with questions, beginning with Thomas, who asked, "Lord, we don't know where you are going, so how can we know the way?" (John 14:5).

The irony of this is that Jesus had been telling them where He was going. He had, in fact, told them three times that He was going to the cross to fulfill His rescue mission on our behalf. Now, in the upper room, He adds that this will result in a new, eternal place for them in the Father's house.

Not inappropriately, Thomas wants to know how we can get there, and Jesus's answer carries the biggest idea of all: it is only through Him.

He had alluded to this earlier in John 10 in His "good shepherd" teaching when He said, "I am the gate; whoever enters through me will be saved. They will come in and go out, and find pasture" (John 10:9). Peace, rest, provision all come only through Him.

Later, when speaking to a different crowd, one of Jesus's followers, Simon Peter, made the same point, saying, "Salvation is found in no one else, for there is no other name under heaven given to mankind by which we must be saved" (Acts 4:12).

Over and over again, the Scriptures affirm that there is one way. One door. One name. Only in Jesus can we experience forgiveness, restoration, and relationship with the Father.

The point? We all start our journeys from different places, at different times, for different reasons. We take different paths. But all of those paths, billions of them, converge at one door. As you share your story with someone, remember to share not only what is unique (your own path) but also what is not unique (where all the paths ultimately converge). Remember that the people you care about likely will have to find and follow a different route than yours, but that at the end of our journeys, we must all pass through the same door.

Lord, thank you for bringing me along my path and through the door into your family. Without your guidance as a Good Shepherd, I would have wandered forever astray. Give me your shepherd's heart for the paths that others are walking along, caring and understanding, but also calling and guiding them home. Amen.

ACTIVITY: Record

Based on your reflections yesterday, make some notes about the process by which you came to faith. There was a sequence of events. List them, in order. Yours might look something like this:

> I grew up going to church and Sunday school and my parents read me Bible stories and said prayers with me by my bedside. As a teenager, I went my own way and drifted far from the things I had been taught. In college, however, the Lord made me aware of how lost and broken and needy I was. I turned to Jesus and asked Him to save me from my sin and myself.

You might tell a similar story, but then tell of some times when you wandered away from the faith, only to find your way back. Or you might have first heard about Christ at a camp, or as an adult. You might have had a sudden conversion centered around some dramatic events in your life, or it might have been a slow process, with steps forward, backward, and sideways before you arrived at faith in Christ. Whatever the sequence of events, this is your story. And no one can tell it but you.

Don't worry about writing a composed essay; you'll do that on Saturday. For today, just make some notes, even bullet-style.

Just get the process and sequence down.

HOW?
TELLING YOUR STORY

DAY 4 • WEDNESDAY

THEME: Missionaries, Mentors, and Models

FOCUS: Record. List the people who helped you get here.

1 Corinthians 4:14–17

> I am writing this not to shame you but to warn you as my dear children. Even if you had ten thousand guardians in Christ, you do not have many fathers, for in Christ Jesus I became your father through the gospel. Therefore I urge you to imitate me. For this reason I have sent to you Timothy, my son whom I love, who is faithful in the Lord. He will remind you of my way of life in Christ Jesus, which agrees with what I teach everywhere in every church.

Devotional Thoughts

You didn't travel alone along your path to Jesus. You had help, even before you were aware you needed it. Long before you were born, let alone spiritually searching, there were followers of Christ building the foundations of the church and sharing the good news of Christ. They left maps and supplies and rest stops along the routes. Additionally, people directly in your life motivated you to begin your journey. Only you know who they were and how they inspired you.

Along the way, you had guides who kept you moving, got you back onto the trail when you got lost, and guardians who kept you safe from your own foolishness (wandering off or too lazy to keep moving) or from enemies who tried to prevent you from continuing.

You also had mentors. Some were parents or family members, some were teachers or pastors, some were neighbors or friends. But they gave you advice, even when you didn't want it or like it. They cared enough to tell you what you needed to hear, even if it wasn't always what you wanted to hear.

Along the way, you had role models, people who showed you what faith in Christ looks like when put into action. Some never spoke a word about Christ, but their lives shined like lights in darkness. Their example exhibited the fruit of the Holy Spirit (Galatians 5:22–23), even when you didn't know what that phrase meant.

In today's passage, Paul reminds the Christians in Corinth of all the guardians they had in the faith. He also reminds them how important it is to have a spiritual father (or mother), a mentor who deeply inspires and shapes their spiritual lives. He then sends Timothy to provide them with further instruction and pastoral guidance, but also to remind them of the way Paul lived out his faith as a model for them to emulate.

Missionaries, mentors, and models: God uses many people to influence our journey in many ways. Who were yours?

> *Lord, thank you for all of the people you sent to guide me along the path to you. Forgive me for those who I misunderstood, failed to appreciate, or even resented, for they came in your name and helped to bring me safely home. Help me to be your representative to others, so that they too may be drawn to your heart. Amen.*

ACTIVITY: Record

Based on your reflections Monday and your notes yesterday about the process or timeline, make some notes about some of the people that were significant in bringing you to faith or in building your faith in the time since you trusted Christ. As we saw in today's devotion, none of us got here alone. The walk of faith is a social, communal faith, a faith of relationships. God brought missionaries, mentors, and role models into your life. Only you know who they were or are, but they are an essential part of your story.

Don't worry about writing a composed essay—you'll do that on Saturday. For today, just make some notes, even bullet-style.

Just record who these people were and their significance to your story.

HOW?
TELLING YOUR STORY

DAY 5 • THURSDAY

THEME: Twists and Turns

FOCUS: Record. Identify the moment, or moments, when you came to faith.

Ephesians 1:11–14

In him we were also chosen, having been predestined according to the plan of him who works out everything in conformity with the purpose of his will, in order that we, who were the first to put our hope in Christ, might be for the praise of his glory. And you also were included in Christ when you heard the message of truth, the gospel of your salvation. When you believed, you were marked in him with a seal, the promised Holy Spirit, who is a deposit guaranteeing our inheritance until the redemption of those who are God's possession—to the praise of his glory.

Devotional Thoughts

Some of us can mark our faith journey with specific moments and dates: a decision for Christ followed by baptism, or a particular moment when, hearing the gospel, it just made sense for the first time. There are other significant moments when we experienced a sense of God's presence: the times we responded to an altar call, prayed a prayer at a conference, or watched a gospel-based television program. Perhaps even when we first started going to church.

For others—maybe for most of us—there have also been low points: valleys of doubt, moral failures, disobedience, rebellion. There have been times that we walked away from God, ignored Him or tried to shut out His voice, gave up worship or prayer. But most of us can remember bright spots as well: moments of clarity, repentance, and renewal.

The great encouragement of Simon Peter's story was that it had twists and turns, advances and retreats, moments of triumph and failure. And that is encouraging, because if that could be true of Peter, the leader of the apostles, how much more could it be true of us?

Your story also has moments: highs and lows, turning points and stumbles. Particularly, as we journey through this devotional month, there must be times you can recall when your hope became clear and convincing.

In today's passage, we are reminded that throughout those twists and turns, Christ is with us, working out everything to lead us to Him.

Lord, as the hymn "Amazing Grace" says, "Through many dangers, toils, and snares I have already come." It was all by your grace that I survived the journey to you. Help me to honestly recall my journey, not to bring credit to myself or to somehow glorify my wrongdoing, but to acknowledge that when I was weak and foolish, you were faithful and strong. Give me the grace to see others who are wandering and struggling as you saw me. Amen.

ACTIVITY: Record

Based on your reflections this week, make some notes about when you first realized or acknowledged your faith in Christ.

For some of you, faith grew gradually. If you were raised in church, you might not be able to point to a specific moment in time—you just always believed and gradually came to accept it. Fair enough, that's an answer—and it's a wonderful answer. All of us who have wandered far from God wish we had been raised in the safety and joy of our Father's house. But even if you did grow up with faith, there were probably moments, and maybe even a big moment, when you had to decide to make that faith your own. It might have been a time of testing, or a profession of faith in a church service. For many of us, there were almost certainly specific moments when you said in effect, Yes, I believe and I am a Christian. Only you know when those moments occurred, but they are an essential part of your story.

This exercise will be important when you share your faith with someone else, because as they wrestle with making a commitment they may ask you, When did you really know? What does that feel like?

Don't worry about writing a composed essay—you'll do that on Saturday. For today, just make some notes, even bullet-style.

Just record the moment, or moments, when you made the faith your own and decided to be counted among the Christians.

HOW?
TELLING YOUR STORY

DAY 6 • FRIDAY

THEME: Called

FOCUS: Read. Review the notes you made this week.

Romans 8:29–30

For those God foreknew he also predestined to be conformed to the image of his Son, that he might be the firstborn among many brothers and sisters. And those he predestined, he also called; those he called, he also justified; those he justified, he also glorified.

Devotional Thoughts

Take a moment to reflect on what you've written the last few days. The outline of your path to faith should be taking shape. Imagine it like a route across a map from where you began to that narrow door. Now imagine seeing that route from high overhead, like a satellite view tracing a twisting road across the landscape. Think about that. Can you see God's hand in that route?

He's always been there, even when you didn't see Him or didn't care about Him. He prepared the way. He placed people and resources (and challenges) along the way.

Sometimes He called out to you, enticing you to come forward. Sometimes He was behind you, either encouraging in a gentle voice or nudging you to get up and keep moving. He pulled, pushed, and sometimes carried you over the worst stretches of the trail. He posted warning signs at the most dangerous spots, and called to you when you ignored them. Sometimes He let you wander a bit to teach you a lesson before sending help when you got too lost or into too much trouble. He sent companions to walk alongside, to coach you and keep you company.

In today's passage, Paul tells us that God's ultimate purpose is that we become like Jesus. It doesn't always make sense at the ground level, as you're wandering up and down the hills, sometimes trying to follow the trail and sometimes ignoring it. But when you finally arrive at that one door where all the paths converge, you realize that it was all for your good.

Father Brown, the priest-detective in the novels by G. K. Chesterton, echoed God's own voice when he said about a wayward character, "I caught him, with an unseen hook and an invisible line which is long enough to let him wander to the ends of the world, and still to bring him back with a twitch upon the thread." That's you and me, on the end of that thread. And it can be the person(s) with whom you want to share your story.

> *Lord, if I still harbor hurts and resentments over the hard moments in my life, heal my heart. Teach me to be grateful for the moments when I had to rely on you, and to understand the ways that you worked through those moments to bring me to the point where I could pray this prayer today. Fill me with joy for the trials that brought me closer to you and shaped my heart to receive the help of your Spirit. Amen.*

ACTIVITY: Read

Today, read what you wrote in your notes this week. Reflect and pray over what you've recorded. Is it accurate? What did you learn? What insights did you capture?

What surprised you? How do you feel about it? What's most important? What's wonderful? Did you leave anything out, get anything wrong, or misrepresent the truth in any way? Organize your thoughts, make additions, corrections, tweaks, because tomorrow you take a mini-retreat to write your faith story.

HOW?
TELLING YOUR STORY

DAY 7 • SATURDAY

THEME: What He Has Done for Me

FOCUS: Retreat and Write. Compose your faith story.

Psalm 66:16

> Come and hear, all you who fear God; let me tell you what he has done for me.

Devotional Thoughts

Today is a retreat day, which means you take time to pray and write.

Begin by reflecting on and praying over today's Scripture, Psalm 66:16. Let it sink deeply into your heart and mind so that it guides your hand as you write today.

"Come and hear . . ." This verse begins with an invitation. It's the same invitation that you are offering to the person(s) with whom you are preparing to share your faith. You can't compel them to act. You can't make them begin their journey in search of that narrow door. But you can invite them to listen.

". . . all you who fear God . . ." Now, you might say that the person you're reaching out to doesn't fear God—that's the reason you want to share with them. But remember what we've learned this week: The Holy Spirit is the one who must ultimately bring them to faith in Jesus. We also learned that God, in an infinite variety of ways, jumpstarts our journeys. Sometimes the motivation is intellectual, sometimes emotional; sometimes it's love, sometimes it's fear; sometimes it's longing for something beautiful, sometimes it's rejection of what's ugly. But God gets us up and moving. Pray that in ways this person does not fully understand, the Holy Spirit would motivate them to begin moving toward understanding and respect for God.

". . . let me tell you what [God] has done for me." This is exactly what this devotional journey is all about. It's not telling someone what to do, or what God has done or not done for them. It's sharing the reasons for the hope that you have, which is grounded in what God has done for you.

Today you begin putting that story together. It's a story in which you are not the main character, God is. It's a humble tale of those who always loved you, even when you didn't deserve it or know it. It's a story of grace.

> *Lord, as I write my story today, let it be full of praise for you. You have done such great things for me, and I want the story of my life to be an eyewitness testimony to mercy, grace, and blessings. Whatever my circumstances today, I am rich in your grace, not because I deserve it but because of your love and power. Amen.*

ACTIVITY: Retreat and Write

Today, you're going to take a mini-retreat to write. This may be difficult if you're not used to solitary time to reflect and write. But give it a try. How do you find the time, with all of your busy commitments? Where do you go where you won't be interrupted or distracted? How long will it take? Because all of us have such different circumstances, there's no single answer. You'll have to figure that out in the context of your life right now. But find some space and time to spend an hour or two of focused time.

Also, writing is challenging, and it's more challenging for some than others. And even for those who do find it easy to write, this isn't an easy assignment. Still, my advice is to ask God's help in figuring it out. Then do your best.

Go back over the notes that you reviewed yesterday, and look at the other entries. Drawing from that material, compose a short letter or essay telling your faith story. It helps most writers to visualize a specific person for whom they're writing. Although you may ultimately share your story with many people, start as though you're talking to one person. It'll help you focus your thoughts. Remember, you aren't publishing your memoir, you're opening your heart and life so that someone can understand how you came to know Jesus.

Week One Retreat
Tips for Writing Your Faith Story

- The most important thing you can do is to be authentic. Don't write fiction, and don't bend the truth. The person you're sending this to knows you, and while the point is to share with them details they don't know, they'll be able to detect if this doesn't sound and feel like the "you" that they really know. In that case, you'll look dishonest and manipulative. That would undermine the whole point of sharing your faith in Christ.

- Don't resort to theatrics and extremes. You're not writing a novel or movie script where you need to pump up the drama. Again, that will only come off as manipulative. Tell the truth, no more and no less. God will bless truth-sharing, and it will resonate with the reader. Even if they don't agree with you, they will respect you being honest and real and even vulnerable.

- Don't share inappropriate or unnecessary details. This isn't the time or place for confession or counseling. There are private parts of your life that can and should remain private. If there are some delicate or even offensive elements in your story that contributed to how you came to faith, find a way to share enough so that the reader understands what happened, but not more than they need to know to see the connection with the development of your faith.

- Don't exaggerate your conversion to make yourself out to be the next apostle Paul. That goes both ways: don't make yourself out to be worse than you really were before you started following Christ or better than you actually are today.

- How long should this be? As short as possible to tell the story. This doesn't have to be book length, or even chapter length. It could be a page, or a few pages. The purpose isn't to detail your autobiography, it's to share the trajectory of your life and how you came to be a Christian.

- Keep it simple. No elaborate sentence constructions, complex words, or flashy stylistic elements. Imagine sitting with the person that you want to share with, and hear them asking you to tell them how you became a Christian. Picture them really listening to you answer the question for five or maybe even ten minutes. What would you say? Write that down.

WHY?
REASONS YOU BELIEVE

DAY 8 • SUNDAY

THEME: Spirit and Truth

FOCUS: Worship. Rest and trust in the Lord.

John 4:21–26

"Woman," Jesus replied, "believe me, a time is coming when you will worship the Father neither on this mountain nor in Jerusalem. You Samaritans worship what you do not know; we worship what we do know, for salvation is from the Jews. Yet a time is coming and has now come when the true worshipers will worship the Father in the Spirit and in truth, for they are the kind of worshipers the Father seeks. God is spirit, and his worshipers must worship in the Spirit and in truth."

The woman said, "I know that Messiah" (called Christ) "is coming. When he comes, he will explain everything to us."

Then Jesus declared, "I, the one speaking to you—I am he."

Devotional Thoughts

It's the Lord's Day again, so take a break from writing and focus on worship. This might be difficult. You want to do something, to stay on top of this project, to keep it moving forward to completion. Taking a break seems unnecessary.

But that approach misses the point. Worship isn't taking a break from evangelism, mission, theology, or any other spiritual endeavor. The work of the gospel doesn't begin in worship, it ends in worship. Worship isn't a useful tool to the spread of the good news, it's the purpose. We seek to bring others into God's family so that we will be able to someday worship together alongside believers of all the ages.

When we worship today, we orient ourselves in that direction and receive an imperfect taste of the perfect worship to come in order to sustain us along our journey. Your hope for the person with whom you want to share your faith is that they will join you along the journey toward that ultimate fellowship with God and His rejoicing creation.

In our Scripture today, we are reminded that authentic worship is directed toward and grounded in Jesus Christ. As Jesus tells the Samaritan woman, despite the differences between the Jews and her people, Christ's true followers will worship Him "in the Spirit and in truth." It's worth reflecting on that today as you enjoy worship, because those are two necessary ingredients for this project. For you to share the reasons for your faith, you will need to have the guidance of the Holy Spirit and to know and speak the truth. It's no coincidence that those are the components of genuine worship.

Grow your faith, pointed and purposed toward the worship of Jesus Christ in Spirit and in truth, so that you can offer it as a gift to someone else.

> *Lord, keep me from worshiping an idea or an ideology. By the Holy Spirit, let me worship you. Not as a means to an end, but because it is right and appropriate for a creature to give thanks and worship the Creator, and for your children to love and adore you. Let me give my heart to you in imitation of how you gave everything to me. Amen.*

ACTIVITY: Worship

You don't need to do anything else today other than go to church and worship. But it's also about trust. Sometimes we work at our faith like we work at our jobs, as if everything depends on us. Worship is an acknowledgment that our lives, success, and happiness are ultimately not about or dependent upon us. We do as much as we can and leave the outcomes to God. So, live that rhythm in this devotional journey and preparation to share your faith. Today, you're not "doing nothing." You're doing the most important thing: giving this faith-sharing project to the Lord and asking Him to bless it.

WHY?
REASONS YOU BELIEVE

DAY 9 • MONDAY

THEME: Confident and Sure

FOCUS: Reflect. Ask yourself why you believe.

Hebrews 11:1–3

> Now faith is confidence in what we hope for and assurance about what we do not see. This is what the ancients were commended for. By faith we understand that the universe was formed at God's command, so that what is seen was not made out of what was visible.

Devotional Thoughts

This devotional journey is about sharing your faith with someone you care about. But what is faith? It's one of those words that we use all the time in our religious communities, and we have a general sense of what it means or what we mean when we use it. But if we use a word vaguely or inconsistently, it can lead to confusion and misunderstanding, which is the last thing we want when sharing our faith. So, what, exactly, is faith?

We could check a dictionary, but for followers of Christ the word is defined clearly and succinctly in our devotional Scripture today. Faith, Hebrews tells us, consists of two things.

First, it is confidence in what we hope for. As we said in the introduction, this book is based on 1 Peter 3:15–16 which tells us to always be prepared to give an answer for the hope that you have. Faith is about hope. But not a hope that's merely a vague, general optimism about the future. It is a very specific hope. It is the concrete expectation that the gospel is true, and that Jesus's promises of eternal life are trustworthy. Hebrews 11 tells us that faith is confidence that hope is not in vain. It is an expectation that we can, and should, base our lives upon.

Second, our passage tells us that faith is assurance about what we do not see. Of course, there are all sorts of things that we cannot see that we are assured are true. Not everything that is real is visible in the spectrum of light that human eyes can register. For example, we may never have seen an atom, much less a proton, electron, or quark. But we don't doubt that they exist because we have been assured by reliable experts who have conducted various experiments and equations. We do see the tangible outcomes of those invisible particles, which gives us even greater assurance. We have *faith* regarding them. By the same token, we can have faith in the Trinity (that God is three-yet-one), in angels, and eternal life. Not because we can see them, but because we have been assured by sources that we trust. And we can see their tangible effects in this world.

This devotional journey is about sharing the reasons that you are confident and sure of the invisible realties into which you have placed your ultimate hope.

Lord, I confess that I am not always confident and sure of you or the Scriptures. Teach me to trust in you through the means and methods you have given me to learn your wisdom. Like the father who asked Jesus to heal his son, I cry to you, "Lord, I believe, help my unbelief!" (Mark 9:24). Amen.

ACTIVITY: Reflect

Today, reflect on why you came to have faith in Christ. Last week, you focused on the how, your story, the sequence of events that brought you here. This week, you'll be explaining why you traveled down that path and what drove you. What convinced your mind to believe that the good news of Jesus is true? What moved your heart to know, deep down inside? What has God done in your life to show you that He is real and He is Lord and deserves your trust?

Pray for insight and honesty, because we aren't always honest with ourselves, imagining ourselves to be smarter and more heroic than we are. As you reflect on why you came to be a disciple of Jesus Christ, jot down some simple notes in your journal. They'll be helpful for your exercises this week.

WHY?
REASONS YOU BELIEVE

DAY 10 • TUESDAY

THEME: Clear and Reasonable

FOCUS: Record. List some of the reasons your mind is convinced.

Romans 1:18–20

The wrath of God is being revealed from heaven against all the godlessness and wickedness of people, who suppress the truth by their wickedness, since what may be known about God is plain to them, because God has made it plain to them. For since the creation of the world God's invisible qualities—his eternal power and divine nature—have been clearly seen, being understood from what has been made, so that people are without excuse.

Devotional Thoughts

Yesterday, we talked about our confidence in what cannot be seen with the human eye. In fact, there are a lot of things that we can't see with our eyes or measure with a device, but that we know, with great confidence, by their effects. We can't peer into a mother's heart to see or measure her love for her children, but we can clearly see that love by the things she does and the effects it has in the lives of her children.

As we saw in Colossians 1, the source of all things is what the gospel of John calls in Greek the *logos*, which we translate as "the Word." God's "Word" is His Son, the second person of the Trinity, who creates, sustains, and rules over everything.

> In the beginning was the Word, and the Word was with God, and the Word was God. He was with God in the beginning. Through him all things were made; without him nothing was made that has been made. In him was life, and that life was the light of all mankind. The light shines in the darkness, and the darkness has not overcome it. (John 1:1–5)

Although we cannot see "the Word" in His pure form, we have seen Him in flesh in this world as Jesus of Nazareth, the Christ.

> *Lord, you have clearly created the universe and placed me into it. I know that your handiwork and the effects of your kingdom are all around me. But there are so many distractions, so many things that keep me from seeing clearly. Help me focus, see, and know. Shine the light of your truth into the dark places of this world and my own life so that that I might realize the grandeur and genius of your lordship over all things. Amen.*

ACTIVITY: Record

Based on your reflections yesterday, make some notes about what convinced your mind that Christianity was true. Many aren't comfortable discussing the intellectual, rational basis of our faith and some even mistakenly think that reason and faith are incompatible opposites. Belief in Jesus, however, is a fact-based, intellectual faith. For example, among other things we believe that God really exists, that Jesus was born to a virgin named Mary in Bethlehem sometime around 3 or 4 BC, that He was put to death by the Roman government, that He rose from the dead on the third day, that He commissioned apostles to spread the news and that they were among the authors of the Bible, and that if we believe and follow Him then we will inherit eternal life when we die. To be a follower of Christ is not to believe that these are mere opinions that comfort us but may or may not be true. It (at least minimally) is to be intellectually convinced that these and other claims are rational, historical facts. Granted, being a believer in Jesus is not only that, but it's never less than that.

And, by the way, it's OK to believe something because a trustworthy person told you that it's true. In fact, our entire legal system and most of our science is based on believing the testimony of trustworthy people. We believe Jesus rose (and everything we know about Him) because the apostles said so.

So, somewhere along the line, your mind became convinced of the truth of Christianity. Why?

Jot down some of those reasons. You don't need to explain or defend them like a pastor or professor, just list them.

WHY? REASONS YOU BELIEVE

DAY 11 • WEDNESDAY

THEME: A Burning Heart

FOCUS: Record. List some of the things that moved your heart to Christ.

Luke 24:30–32

> When he was at the table with them, he took bread, gave thanks, broke it and began to give it to them. Then their eyes were opened and they recognized him, and he disappeared from their sight. They asked each other, "Were not our hearts burning within us while he talked with us on the road and opened the Scriptures to us?"

Devotional Thoughts

Most of us can remember being bored during a sermon, Bible study, or theology class. On plenty of Mondays we haven't been able to remember what the previous day's sermon was about. We only remember it being dull, or feeling confused. Many of us have nodded off during a particularly dry presentation of some doctrine or Bible story.

Sometimes that's the fault of the preachers or teachers. Any of us who do that kind of work are sometimes guilty of taking the Bible—the world's most exciting book—and making it dull. Some of us aren't the most gifted communicators.

No matter how weak the presentation, though, we all have a responsibility to pay attention to the Scriptures. If it really is what we say it is, and as important as we believe it is, shouldn't we make the effort as if our lives depended on knowing and understanding and implementing God's Word in our lives? In fact, our lives actually do depend on it.

Our passage today comes after the risen Christ meets two of His disciples on the first resurrection Sunday. They are walking away from Jerusalem with heavy hearts, despondent over what they are thinking is the tragedy of the crucifixion, because they haven't heard yet about the resurrection. He comes alongside them, but His identity is temporarily cloaked. As they walk along, this stranger who isn't really a stranger unpacks the entire Old Testament for them, explaining how it all pointed to Jesus Christ, the beginning and end of all things. When they reach the inn in Emmaus, Jesus reveals His identity and then disappears. They are in wonder and think about the teaching they had just received over the last few hours. "They asked each other, 'Were not our hearts burning within us while he talked with us on the road and opened the Scriptures to us?'" (Luke 24:32).

Think of that: hearing the complete story of the world's creation and meaning, its beginning and purpose and end, decoding and unpacking how God is restoring and redeeming a fallen cosmos, caused their hearts to burn within them.

Sure, your pastor or professor might not be the most dynamic communicator. But can we always blame our boredom on his or her poor presentation? Or have we allowed our hearts to grow so cold and hard that God's truth can't warm them?

> *Lord, forgive me for the times when I have found the Bible boring, or when I neglected it, or when I ignored it because I was afraid of its truth and ashamed of my actions. Let the story of your love for this world light a fire in my heart as I gain confidence in the beauty and power of your Scriptures. Amen.*

ACTIVITY: Record

Based on your reflections Monday, make some notes about what moved your heart to believe that the Christian faith was true. Yesterday, we saw that trusting Christ is never less than being intellectually convinced that the gospel is true, but that it's more than only that. Much of the time we put hope and trust in things (and people) because our heart is convinced. We have rational reasons for believing that our families love us (such as by the things that they do), but it is ultimately our hearts rather than our minds that are convinced of their love for us. You know that your house is your home, for instance, inasmuch as you live there, and your stuff is there. But when you return from a trip and drive up your street and into your driveway, it's your heart that tells you that you're home. Our minds makes a space for belief, but our hearts fill that space with conviction.

So, what in the gospel so touched your heart that it would be impossible for you to stop believing? What has convinced your heart so that you have a hope that you would bet your life on? What so captured your heart that you would sacrifice pleasure and security in this life for the promise of the next one?

What caused your heart to put such trust in Jesus Christ that you would even take up your own cross to follow Him?

Jot down some of those reasons. You don't need to explain or defend them like a pastor or professor, just list them.

WHY?
REASONS YOU BELIEVE

DAY 12 • THURSDAY

THEME: Astonished and Ashamed

FOCUS: Record. List experiences that have proven God's power in your life.

Luke 5:1–11

One day as Jesus was standing by the Lake of Gennesaret, the people were crowding around him and listening to the word of God. He saw at the water's edge two boats, left there by the fishermen, who were washing their nets. He got into one of the boats, the one belonging to Simon, and asked him to put out a little from shore. Then he sat down and taught the people from the boat.

When he had finished speaking, he said to Simon, "Put out into deep water, and let down the nets for a catch."

Simon answered, "Master, we've worked hard all night and haven't caught anything. But because you say so, I will let down the nets."

When they had done so, they caught such a large number of fish that their nets began to break. So they signaled their partners in the other boat to come and help them, and they came and filled both boats so full that they began to sink.

When Simon Peter saw this, he fell at Jesus's knees and said, "Go away from me, Lord; I am a sinful man!" For he and all his companions were astonished at the catch of fish they had taken, and so were James and John, the sons of Zebedee, Simon's partners.

Then Jesus said to Simon, "Don't be afraid; from now on you will fish for people." So they pulled their boats up on shore, left everything and followed him.

Devotional Thoughts

Obviously, people are not machines. Our humanity is a complex thing, meaning that it is made up of interlocking components. For us to really believe something, our minds have to be convinced and our emotions engaged. That's what the last two days have been about. But there's at least one other dimension to genuine belief or true faith: experience. We might intellectually know that someone loves us, and we might be emotionally committed to that belief. But what makes us absolutely certain of their love is the million ways, great and small that they tangibly touch our lives giving us the experience of their love.

In our passage today, Peter has an experience that convinces him, without a doubt, of Jesus's identity. At this point, Peter has been following Jesus as a teacher. He is emotionally committed to Jesus. He has seen Jesus do miracles and preach sermons.

But then Jesus does something that tangibly demonstrates His love and power in Peter's life. Peter and his fishing crew have spent a long, hard night and they have nothing to show for it. Peter is sleep-deprived, and every muscle in his body aches. Now he has to clean up the boats, repair the equipment, and figure out how to pay today's bills. Jesus tells Peter to go back out. Peter appears hesitant, but he respects Jesus, so he does as Jesus says. Inside, though, Peter is full of doubt. Then Jesus does a miracle for Peter, something that shows His power over nature (remember, all things are under His authority).

And that is the moment when Peter really, really gets it. He realizes who Jesus really is, who he himself is, and the immeasurable gap between them. He falls down and confesses that Jesus is

Lord, he is a sinful man, and begs for Jesus to leave him because he isn't worthy to be in Jesus's presence.

At that moment, Peter is ready to begin serving. Jesus will make him a fisher of men.

Today, reflect on how your experiences convinced you that Jesus Christ is Lord.

> *Lord, make me astonished at your love and power, and ashamed of my own sin. But also make me aware of your grace and the inheritance I have in your name. Help me to recall the ways that you have tangibly demonstrated your love and patience and leadership in my life, even when I ignored you or ran from you. Amen.*

ACTIVITY: Record

Based on your reflections from Monday, make some notes about what experiences in your life proved to you that Jesus Christ is Lord.

Over the last two days, you listed the reasons that your mind and heart are convinced. But there's a third element to human belief, beyond rational argument and intuitive emotion: experiences that motivated and validated our faith. Of course, the Bible is full of such experiences: Moses at the burning bush, the Israelites passing through the Red Sea, Elijah and the prophets of Baal, Jonah and the great fish, the apostles' and Jesus's various miracles, the resurrection, Paul on the road to Damascus, and more. In all those cases, people had reasons for belief and even emotional attachments to God, but then God showed up and demonstrated that He was real in their lives, after which there was no going back.

Although our experiences may not have the miraculous drama of those Bible characters, most believers in Jesus will have had some experiences through which God proved that He was real. Because to be a follower of Christ means not just believing an ideology or having deep feelings but to have encountered Christ and to be following Him through this world. Every day is another opportunity for an encounter with and demonstration of God's provision and care for us. And if we open our eyes, we will see many ways that He meets our needs and surprises us with His leadership and direct involvement in our lives.

So, what has God done in your life that has convinced you to follow and trust Him?

Jot down some of those reasons. You don't need to explain or defend them like a pastor or professor, just list them.

WHY?
REASONS YOU BELIEVE

DAY 13 • FRIDAY

THEME: A Gift

FOCUS: Read. Review the notes you made this week.

Ephesians 2:8-9

> For it is by grace you have been saved, through faith—and this is not from yourselves, it is the gift of God—not by works, so that no one can boast.

Devotional Thoughts

Let's look back at what we've learned this week. Faith is being convinced that what we cannot see is true and reliable. We come to that assurance because of what God has reasonably demonstrated to our minds. We feel confident because of how God has moved our hearts by fully engaging our emotions.

And we are willing to bet our lives because of the ways God has proven himself to us again and again through experience.

What does all of that have in common? God acts and we respond. He doesn't magically zap us and make us believe. God doesn't ignore us, sit back and wait for us to want Him, search for Him, and work to find Him. He initiates our faith by making the first moves, and we react. He touches us in the deepest places of our hearts, and changes our lives in undeniable ways.

Our faith is a gift. We aren't believers because we're smarter than those who don't believe. We don't believe because we're better people. We don't believe because we're more curious, disciplined, or educated. We believe because He reached out to us, not the other way around. So, we have no basis for boasting.

That also means that we have no basis for looking down on others. As you prepare to share your faith with someone that you care about, remember that except for the gift of His grace, you would be without faith as well.

Why you? Certainly, there are other people that God could have called and given the gift of faith. But He wanted you. Why? God only knows. But consider this: maybe, just maybe, He gave you faith so that you could share it with the person you are preparing for this month.

> *Lord, never let me be or appear to be arrogant in my faith. May I never be a stumbling block to anyone else by acting as if I deserved your gift of salvation. May my heart, demeanor, words, and tone be humble, grateful, and full of the same grace for others that you gave to me. Amen.*

ACTIVITY: Read

Today, read what you wrote in your journal and other notes this week. Reflect and pray over what you've recorded. Is it accurate? What did you learn? What insights did you capture? What surprised you? How do you feel about it?

What's most important? What's wonderful? Did you leave anything out, get anything wrong, or misrepresent the truth in any way? Organize your thoughts, make additions, corrections, and tweaks, because tomorrow you take a mini-retreat to write the reasons for your faith.

WHY?
REASONS YOU BELIEVE

DAY 14 • SATURDAY

THEME: Do You Need to See?

FOCUS: Retreat and Write. Share the reasons for
your faith.

John 20:26–29

A week later his disciples were in the house again, and Thomas
was with them. Though the doors were locked, Jesus came and
stood among them and said, "Peace be with you!" Then he said to
Thomas, "Put your finger here; see my hands. Reach out your hand
and put it into my side. Stop doubting and believe."
Thomas said to him, "My Lord and my God!"
Then Jesus told him, "Because you have seen me, you have
believed; blessed are those who have not seen and yet have believed."

Devotional Thoughts

This week, you've been reflecting on the questions, Why do you believe? Why are you confident in what you hope for and sure of what
you cannot see? You've asked why your mind has been convinced,
why your heart has been moved, and what you've learned through
experience that has led you to faith. Hopefully, your prayer, reflec-
tion, and journaling this week have given you clear, and maybe
even surprising, insights and answers to those questions.

Some of us come to faith more easily than others. If you're naturally skeptical, you might look down on people who are convinced too quickly. Certainly, that's how the apostle Thomas may have felt. The other apostles had seen the risen Jesus and believed. Thomas had at least two problems with that. First, although the others had seen, he hadn't. He wouldn't accept the claim of the resurrection only on the testimony of his brother apostles. That's relevant for us today, because we accept the fact of the resurrection on their claim—obviously we weren't there. They saw, gave witness throughout the rest of their lives, and some recorded what they had seen in the New Testament. That's all Thomas had, and really all we have today. Second, Thomas wanted to examine the body, to verify Jesus's identity through the scars of His execution. Thomas needed evidence.

Then Jesus shows up. In mercy, He gives Thomas what he needs to be convinced. But He praises those whose faith comes through a trusting heart and trust in the testimony of His apostles.

The person with whom you share your story might be a "doubting Thomas," or maybe you yourself were. The Lord can work with that. In fact, a faith that has grown through investigation or been tested by doubt can often better equip a Christ-follower for the struggles of life or challenges of evangelism. Tradition tells us that Thomas went on to bring the faith to India and died a martyr's death there. Perhaps touching Jesus's wounds gave him a confidence for that mission. But still, most of the others in that room believed without needing to see and touch, and Jesus told Thomas, "blessed are those who have not seen and yet have believed." Jesus praises childlike faith. You could, and perhaps should, use this month to prepare a series of arguments to convince someone. But throughout the Bible, and countless times since then, God has greatly blessed those who heard the gospel and believed because the Holy Spirit touched their heart and helped them recognize it as beautiful and good.

Lord, as I try to explain the reasons for my faith, may I be speaking of true faith. May my relationship with you be grounded in more than just arguments and evidence. May it be a living relationship with you based on trust and commitment. Help me to fully experience and share the trust that I have in you. Amen.

ACTIVITY: Retreat and Write

Today, you're going to take another mini-retreat to write. Where and how did you do your retreat last Saturday? Was that place and method effective? Did it work for you? Then do that again. If it didn't, why not? Try something different this week. Having done this last week, you know what the exercise involves. Be innovative and experiment. But use wisdom and self-discipline, because you don't want to feel like you wasted a day. With God's help, figure it out and do your best.

Go back over the notes that you reviewed yesterday, and the other entries in your journal. Drawing from that material, compose a short letter or essay explaining the reasons for your faith. We organized the exercises around your mind, your heart, and your experiences. You might use those as categories, or blend them together if it's feeling too much like a three-point sermon. Find your voice, and keep in mind the person with whom you'll be sharing it. How long should it be? No longer than you need to explain your reasons to the person you have in mind. You're opening your heart and life so that someone can understand why you became a Christian.

Week Two Retreat
Tips for Sharing Your Reasons for Faith

- You don't have to stick with the "mind, heart, and experience" formula. That was a helpful way to organize your thoughts, but it might not be the best way to present them to the person you have in mind.

- On the other hand, there's nothing wrong with that formula. It's understandable, and if it's authentic for you and if you don't think it will be a barrier to the person you have in mind, then go for it.

- The most important thing is to be genuine. Let it be your own voice. The person who reads this doesn't want to think you simply downloaded information from the internet to pass on. They want to hear you. Even if they don't agree with your reasons, they'll respect that they were yours.

- Speak and frame this in the first person. Use "I" and "me" and "my." Say, "I came to believe that Jesus really lived, died, and rose again because I . . ." Or say, "It touched me deeply when . . ." Or, "My heart tells me that . . ."

- Avoid lecturing. Don't talk down. Don't tell your reader what they are supposed to believe, or why what they believe is wrong. Of course, I'm not saying that everyone is right. That's not the point of this. But if you want them to keep reading and to keep the conversation going, speak from your perspective. At this point, your goal isn't to convince, it's to be genuinely heard. Once you've been heard, then the Holy Spirit can work on the convincing.

- Keep it short. Hit the highlights. Remember, your goal is to be heard and to keep the conversation alive. Boring or overwhelming them shuts down the conversation.

WHAT?
YOUR FAITH STATEMENT

DAY 15 • SUNDAY

THEME: The Fruitful Word

FOCUS: Worship. Rest and trust in the Lord.

2 Timothy 3:16–17

> All Scripture is God-breathed and is useful for teaching, rebuking, correcting and training in righteousness, so that the servant of God may be thoroughly equipped for every good work.

Devotional Thoughts

Over the last two weeks, you've reflected on how and why you came to faith. This week, you're going to reflect upon the substance of that faith.

That means that you're going to engage with and consider the Bible. That can be frightening: what if the person you care for and share with doesn't like or agree with it? What if it offends or bores them? What if they reject it, or you? What if they are not convinced by it?

Today's Scripture is a wonderful promise: The Scriptures are breathed by God and profitable for those who access their wisdom.

It might not have the effect that you desire, at least not immediately or visibly. Someone might very well reject it or be offended by it. And certainly someone might reject you and your presentation.

But the inspired Scriptures have the potential and promise to be effective in four ways. First, the Scriptures are profitable for instruction. Because God is the source, we can learn and discover things about ourselves and our world that we could not know any other way. He is the source of all true knowledge, and therefore we can benefit from its instruction.

Second, the Bible is profitable for "rebuking." What does that mean? It deals with challenging someone whose behavior is going in a sin-based, self-destructive direction. It calls them to go a better way.

Third, we find the Scriptures profitable for correcting. Where rebuking has to do with addressing harmful behavior, correcting deals with challenging wrong ideas.

Finally, the Bible is profitable for "training in righteousness." Because *righteousness* refers to right standing or right relationship, instruction in righteousness involves training us to live in right relationship with God.

As you prepare for this week by worshiping today, remember that Christ is King, that the gospel is true, that the world is changed by it, and that Scriptures are God-breathed and profitable.

> *Lord, I am thankful that the Bible has produced fruit in my life. I may not have known or understood it at the time, but I can see now that you were challenging me and equipping me to walk with you. As I reflect this week on what I believe, let the truths of the Bible come to my mind so that I can clearly articulate the truth about you. Amen.*

ACTIVITY: Worship

This week, you're going to study, reflect, and write about what you believe. You'll be using the Apostle's Creed to organize your faith statement. For nearly two thousand years, many Christian traditions have been reciting this most basic summary of our faith in worship. Whether or not your church uses the Creed in worship today, reflect on it for a few moments on your own:

> I believe in God, the Father almighty, creator of heaven and earth. I believe in Jesus Christ, God's only Son, our Lord, who was conceived by the Holy Spirit, born of the Virgin Mary, suffered under Pontius Pilate, was crucified, died, and was buried; he descended to the dead. On the third day he rose again; he ascended into heaven, he is seated at the right hand of the Father, and he will come to judge the living and the dead. I believe in the Holy Spirit, the holy catholic Church, the communion of saints, the forgiveness of sins, the resurrection of the body, and the life everlasting. Amen.

Prepare for this week by setting yourself free by acknowledging and worshiping the incarnate, living truth—Christ Jesus, the Lord.

WHAT?
YOUR FAITH STATEMENT

DAY 16 • MONDAY

THEME: Solid Food

FOCUS: Reflect. Ponder and summarize what
you believe.

Hebrews 5:11–14

> We have much to say about this, but it is hard to make it clear to
> you because you no longer try to understand. In fact, though by this
> time you ought to be teachers, you need someone to teach you the
> elementary truths of God's word all over again. You need milk, not
> solid food! Anyone who lives on milk, being still an infant, is not
> acquainted with the teaching about righteousness. But solid food
> is for the mature, who by constant use have trained themselves to
> distinguish good from evil.

Devotional Thoughts

The Christian faith requires the heart, but it's not just feelings
and sentiments. We believe that some things are true, that they
actually happened.

In recent years, followers of Christ have not always done a
good job of teaching the substance of our beliefs. We've empha-
sized feelings, passion, and experience. All of that is important,
as we've seen the last few weeks. But it can't stop there. It has

to lead us to truth. Christ-followers should be confident, happy, peaceful, and kind. But the definition of a Christian is someone who believes some very specific things about Jesus and follows Him. Those qualities are the resulting characteristics, what Jesus and Paul call the fruit of our faith—not our faith itself. At some point, we have to say what it is that we believe and stand for. At some point, as Peter says, we have to be prepared to give a reason for the hope we have.

When asked that question, we can't answer that we are hopeful because we are hopeful. Our hope is grounded in our belief in some actual truth. This week, we are going to reflect and even research those beliefs.

The apostles had a notion of "the good deposit," a core of teaching entrusted to them by Christ. With this good deposit, they were supposed to produce results. They were to go into the world, teaching what He commanded, making disciples, and so on.

> *Lord, help me to grow to maturity in my belief. Where my understanding of the Scriptures and their teachings is shallow, make it deep. Where I am of poor understanding, make me wise. Where I am weary, make me curious to learn. Where I am in error, correct me. May I believe in the truth so that I can share it with others. Amen.*

ACTIVITY: Reflect

Today, reflect on what you believe about Christ. The last two weeks you have focused on your story, the path that brought you here, and what drove you down that path. This week, you're going to work through the substance of your faith. You believe that Jesus Christ is Lord, but what do you mean by that? You believe in the Christian faith, but what does Christian belief consist of? You can't ask someone else to believe in something vague: you have to share what it is you are asking them to believe with you. Pray for insight and clarity, because most of us don't spend much or any time thinking about Bible doctrine. As you reflect on what you believe to be true about Jesus Christ, jot down some simple notes in your journal.

They'll be helpful for your exercises this week.

WHAT?
YOUR FAITH STATEMENT

DAY 17 • TUESDAY

THEME: Myths for Itching Ears

FOCUS: Record. Research and record insights about the Father.

2 Timothy 4:3-4

For the time will come when people will not put up with sound doctrine. Instead, to suit their own desires, they will gather around them a great number of teachers to say what their itching ears want to hear. They will turn their ears away from the truth and turn aside to myths.

Devotional Thoughts

Earlier, you reflected on the Apostles' Creed, which falls into three sections: The Father section, the Son section, and the Spirit section. Today, we reflect on the Father section of the Apostles' Creed:

I believe in God, the Father almighty, creator of heaven and earth.

The Creed begins here because it lays the foundation of our belief and worldview: A Creator who is a person and is almighty. Our faith is not in some impersonal force, some pantheon of gods, or any other alternatives to an almighty personal God.

These competing ideas were the religions, myths, and world-view of the ancient pagans. First the Jews and then the church taught that God is one, that He is a Father, that He is almighty, and that He is the Creator of heaven and earth. Believers lived within societies and cultures that taught all sorts of alternatives, but they stubbornly and courageously stuck with the good news of the Scriptures, even sometimes at the cost of their lives. But ideas similar to these religious alternatives are becoming popular again today. People are sometimes more inclined to believe in forces of nature, of a "god" detached from any real involvement in the world, or of a universe that somehow creates itself.

Believers in Christ are convinced of different and better things. We believe in the true God as He has revealed himself to us in the Bible.

As you reflect upon who God is, bear in mind that the notion of God is not always comforting to everyone. Many people are afraid of Him, or avoiding Him. Think about what you know about God, and don't be surprised if some people may turn away to the gods of this world.

> *Lord, forgive me for those times when I have fallen for, or even preferred, false ideas over the truth of the Scriptures. Help me be a witness to the truth of the gospel and to a solid understanding of your heart. Help me and those around me to not be distracted or deceived by false teachings. Amen.*

ACTIVITY: Record

Today, you're going to do a little reading and research, and record what was interesting or especially meaningful to you.

Again, the summary of Christian belief we will use is the Apostles' Creed. Hundreds of years ago, the Creed emerged as a series of questions and answers asked by a convert at his or her baptism. The convert (called a *catechumen*, one who is studying and learning the faith) would be asked "Do you believe in God the Father, maker of heaven and earth?" and would answer, "I do." When they had affirmed the summary of Christian belief, they would be baptized and accepted as a follower of Christ and member of the church. It's called the Apostles' Creed not because it was written by the apostles but because it was considered a faithful summary of the teaching of the apostles (Peter, Paul, James, John, and the rest).

It's the most basic summary of what Christians actually believe.

The Apostles' Creed is divided into three sections, one that summarizes what we believe about the Father, one for the Son, and one for the Holy Spirit. Again, the section about the Father reads:

I believe in God the Father almighty, creator of heaven and earth.

That's just a few words, but there are a lot of implications packed into them. Do some research online (please see www.MH2U.org for a starting point) and make some notes on the next page about what stands out as particularly important to you, and that you think would be particularly important to the person or persons with whom you're going to share your story.

WHAT?
YOUR FAITH STATEMENT

DAY 18 • WEDNESDAY

THEME: Don't Lose This

FOCUS: Record. Research and record insights about the Son.

2 John 1:6–11

And this is love: that we walk in obedience to his commands. As you have heard from the beginning, his command is that you walk in love.

I say this because many deceivers, who do not acknowledge Jesus Christ as coming in the flesh, have gone out into the world. Any such person is the deceiver and the antichrist.

Watch out that you do not lose what we have worked for, but that you may be rewarded fully. Anyone who runs ahead and does not continue in the teaching of Christ does not have God; whoever continues in the teaching has both the Father and the Son. If anyone comes to you and does not bring this teaching, do not take them into your house or welcome them. Anyone who welcomes them shares in their wicked work.

Devotional Thoughts

Today, we reflect upon the Son section of the Apostles' Creed:

I believe in Jesus Christ, God's only Son, our Lord, who was conceived by the Holy Spirit, born of the Virgin Mary, suffered under Pontius Pilate, was crucified, died, and was buried; he descended to the dead. On the third day he rose again; he ascended into heaven, he is seated at the right hand of the Father, and he will come to judge the living and the dead.

The Son is the second person of the three-in-one God (Trinity). This is the great insight of the Christian faith. The Jews had only the revelation of the Old Testament, and they were right about what it taught: there is one God, the God of Abraham, Isaac, and Jacob, the God of Moses and David and the prophets, the God of Israel.

Through the New Testament, however, we have further revelation about God's nature. Jesus is the Christ, the Messiah. The Old Testament hinted at and foreshadowed a more complete truth: God in His nature is a Trinity of persons. Jesus wasn't just the Messiah, the human Savior of Israel. He was the Son of God, God himself born in flesh as a human being.

Our Scripture today speaks of this truth as essential, undeniable for the Christian faith. To lose this truth is to lose the truth that leads to all truths, the only truth that underlines the message of the gospel. If we lose this, then we lose everything.

Peter declares that the truth of Christ was revealed to him and the other apostles, and that we must all trust their testimony:

> For we did not follow cleverly devised stories when we told you about the coming of our Lord Jesus Christ in power, but we were eyewitnesses of his majesty. He received honor and glory from God the Father when the voice came to him from the Majestic Glory, saying, "This is my Son, whom I love; with him I am well pleased." We ourselves heard this voice that came from heaven when we were with him on the sacred mountain. (2 Peter 1:16–18)

We also have the gospel message as something completely reliable.

> *Lord, I know that the opposition to Jesus and the gospel in this world. It is easy to get confused and led astray. Forgive me when I have not stood upon the truth about you. May I never compromise my faith for false teaching or empty promises. May I never deny you by my words or actions. Amen.*

ACTIVITY: Record

Today, you're going to continue reading and doing research, and record what was interesting or especially meaningful to you.

Again, the section of the Apostles' Creed that summarizes our belief about the Son reads:

> I believe in Jesus Christ, God's only Son, our Lord, who was conceived by the Holy Spirit, born of the Virgin Mary, suffered under Pontius Pilate, was crucified, died, and was buried; he descended to the dead. On the third day he rose again; he ascended into heaven, he is seated at the right hand of the Father, and he will come to judge the living and the dead.

That's a wealth of words, and there's a lot packed into them. What stands out as particularly important to you? What do you think would be particularly important to the person or persons with whom you're going to share your story?

Week 3

WHAT?
YOUR FAITH STATEMENT

DAY 19 • THURSDAY

THEME: False Teachers

FOCUS: Record. Research and record insights about the Holy Spirit.

2 Peter 2:1–3

But there were also false prophets among the people, just as there will be false teachers among you. They will secretly introduce destructive heresies, even denying the sovereign Lord who bought them—bringing swift destruction on themselves. Many will follow their depraved conduct and will bring the way of truth into disrepute. In their greed these teachers will exploit you with fabricated stories. Their condemnation has long been hanging over them, and their destruction has not been sleeping.

Devotional Thoughts

Today, you will learn and reflect on the Holy Spirit section of the Creed:

I believe in the Holy Spirit, the holy catholic Church, the communion of saints, the forgiveness of sins, the resurrection of the body, and the life everlasting. Amen.

There are lots of important ideas in these lines. The Holy Spirit is the third person of the Trinity. He is not merely a "spirit" but a person in the same way that the Father and Son are persons within the Godhead. Thus, the Bible refers to the Holy Spirit as *he*. The other great creed of the Christian faith is the Nicene Creed, which tells us that the Holy Spirit proceeds from the Father and the Son, meaning that He is of equal status to them. John 14:26 and Luke 12:12 tell us that the Holy Spirit teaches us truth.

This is comforting as you prepare what to say and share. This isn't just a contest of intellects and emotions and wills. Because if you are genuinely open to the Holy Spirit's guidance, your will and emotions and words and demeanor will be influenced by Him.

There are important truths implied in this section of the Creed. It is in this section that we confess that we believe in the "holy catholic Church." First, this is the next line after the Holy Spirit because it is the Spirit that forms, guides, animates, and fills the church. The church is "holy" for that reason. It is also "catholic," meaning that it is "universal," in all places, in all centuries, of all races, nations, and languages. And if that church seeks and opens itself to the genuine guidance of the Holy Spirit, it might wander, but over time it will always be brought back.

Today's Scripture reminds us of this reality by pointing out the opposite. There will come false teachers, destructive teachings, and soul-crushing conflicts whenever we ignore the authentic guidance of the Spirit. Such false teachers are trying to disrupt the nature of the church, to make it something else.

Lord, I acknowledge that the truth of your kingdom must be taught and defended from false teaching. And I confess that I have not always done my part to stand up for the truth. Help me to recognize, to embrace, and to stand with your true church. Also, help me to understand the work of your Spirit in all its complexity and richness. Amen.

ACTIVITY: Record

Today, continue reading and doing research, recording what was interesting or especially meaningful to you.

The section of the Apostles' Creed that summarizes our belief about the Holy Spirit reads:

> I believe in the Holy Spirit, the holy catholic [universal] Church [that is, the true Christian church of God's redeemed people in all times and all places], the communion [community, intimate fellowship, participation with] of saints [all those who believe Christ], the forgiveness of sins, the resurrection of the body, and the life everlasting. Amen.

There's a lot packed into these words. Make some notes about what stands out as particularly important to you, and what you think would be particularly important to the person or persons with whom you're going to share.

WHAT?
YOUR FAITH STATEMENT

DAY 20 • FRIDAY

THEME: Maturity

FOCUS: Read. Review the notes you made this week.

Ephesians 4:11–14

> So Christ himself gave the apostles, the prophets, the evange-
> lists, the pastors and teachers, to equip his people for works of
> service, so that the body of Christ may be built up until we all
> reach unity in the faith and in the knowledge of the Son of God
> and become mature, attaining to the whole measure of the full-
> ness of Christ. Then we will no longer be infants, tossed back
> and forth by the waves, and blown here and there by every wind
> of teaching and by the cunning and craftiness of people in their
> deceitful scheming.

Devotional Thoughts

Yesterday, our Scripture talked about the false teachers. Today,
we are reminded that we are blessed to have been given sound
leaders by the Spirit.

But notice their purpose: to build up the church. Paul tells
us that building us up means growing us up. Children are cute,
but they're not supposed to remain children forever. They're
supposed to grow into adults, to grow from immaturity into

maturity. We can't remain infants forever. You're engaging in this devotional month because you want to share your faith with someone who matters to you. You have to have sufficient understanding of your faith before you can share it with someone else. That means more than just biblical knowledge, but it doesn't mean less. In other words, you need to know enough about the substance of belief to share and answer questions. Of course, you don't need to be an expert, able to answer any question. No one expects you to be a pastor or theology professor, but you should know enough to share or mentor or coach someone younger in the faith than yourself.

In 1 Corinthians 3:2, Paul reminds the Corinthian believers, "I gave you milk, not solid food, for you were not yet ready for it. Indeed, you are still not ready." Hebrews 5:12 tells its readers that, "In fact, though by this time you ought to be teachers, you need someone to teach you the elementary truths of God's word all over again. You need milk, not solid food!"

That's why God gives us pastors and teachers, to help us grow up so that we can help others grow. God doesn't want just children, He wants His children to grow up.

> *Lord, forgive me for the times when I didn't appreciate or support church leaders who were doing the work of your gospel. Forgive me for the times when I ignored or criticized them, or failed to respond to their leadership so that I might grow to maturity. As I grow in Christ, wean me from the milk of infancy to the solid food of understanding your Word and learning sound doctrine. Amen.*

ACTIVITY: Read

Today, read what you have written in your journal and other notes this week. Reflect and pray over what you've recorded. Is it accurate? What did you learn? What insights did you capture? What surprised you? How do you feel about it?

What's most important? What's wonderful? Did you leave anything out, get anything wrong, or manipulate the truth in any way? Organize your thoughts, make additions, corrections, and tweaks, because tomorrow you take a mini-retreat to write your faith statement.

WHAT?
YOUR FAITH STATEMENT

DAY 21 • SATURDAY

THEME: Witnesses

FOCUS: Retreat and Write. Compose your
faith statement.

Matthew 28:16–20

Then the eleven disciples went to Galilee, to the mountain where
Jesus had told them to go. When they saw him, they worshiped
him; but some doubted. Then Jesus came to them and said, "All
authority in heaven and on earth has been given to me. Therefore
go and make disciples of all nations, baptizing them in the name
of the Father and of the Son and of the Holy Spirit, and teaching
them to obey everything I have commanded you. And surely I am
with you always, to the very end of the age."

Acts 1:7–8

He said to them: "It is not for you to know the times or dates the
Father has set by his own authority. But you will receive power when
the Holy Spirit comes on you; and you will be my witnesses in Jerusalem, and in all Judea and Samaria, and to the ends of the earth."

Devotional Thoughts

This week, you've been studying and reflecting on the substance of your faith, because if you want to share that faith with someone else, you can't just share how and why you came to believe, you have to share what it is that you do believe.

Our first Scripture today is known as The Great Commission. Jesus "commissioned" us—assigned us a task along with responsibility and His authority to carry it out—to share our faith. But sharing our faith is only one part of the responsibility of our mission. What Jesus actually says is that we are to make disciples and teach them to obey everything He commanded. That's not a process, it's an outcome.

Our second Scripture today contains Jesus's last words before He ascended into heaven (to sit at the right hand of God the Father Almighty). He tells us that the Holy Spirit will make us "witnesses" throughout the world (and over the centuries).

Witnesses testify to what they have seen and know to be true.

Today, you retreat and write. As you do, write with purpose. The point of sharing the substance of your faith is not to debate for debate's sake. It's not to educate for education's sake. Yes, there is a place for apologetics and study, and even times for a good discussion on the substance of issues that matter. But that's not the purpose of sharing what you believe.

The purpose is clear: make disciples. Disciples aren't just students, nor are they just fans or followers. A disciple is someone who develops his or her life along the pattern or model of a master. Disciples study and learn, but they study and learn so they can apply that knowledge to growing up to resemble their master. That's why Jesus adds, "Teaching them to obey everything I have commanded." Disciples don't just *know*, they *do*.

Jesus wants us to be witnesses, meaning that we testify to who Christ is. The way we do that is not just with our words, but with our lives and actions as well. We give witness to the power of Christ by demonstrating that power to change us.

> *Lord, as I sit down to write and try to explain what I believe, make me a witness who testifies to your resurrection and power. Don't let me just lecture or argue. Help me to make disciples and teach them to obey what you have commanded by first being a disciple who obeys. Amen.*

ACTIVITY: Retreat and Write

Today, you're going to take another mini-retreat to write. Where and how did you do your last two retreats? Were those places and methods effective? What worked for you? Then do that again. If something didn't, why not? Try something different this week. Having done this for two weeks, you know what the exercise involves. Be innovative and experiment. But use wisdom and self-discipline, because you don't want to feel like you wasted a day. With God's help, figure it out and do your best.

Go back over the notes that you reviewed yesterday, and the other entries in your journal. Drawing from that material, compose a short letter or essay explaining your faith statement.

Remember, the purpose of this is for you to share with someone which aspects of Christian doctrine are especially meaningful to you. The goal is that they would read this and better understand the reasons you have for your hope in Christ.

Week Three Retreat
Tips for Sharing Your Reasons for Faith

- Your faith statement can take many forms. There's no one right format or voice. In fact, there are probably as many right ways to express your faith as there are personalities and life stories. For example, Greg Smith is a seminary-educated writer who has spent more than thirty years working in apologetics, ministry to college students, and strategic communications. When he shares his faith, he expresses himself in a way that arises from that life experience. He uses more technical language and has his thoughts organized in neat bullet points. Joy Anderson is a grandmother with a giant heart full of love, who has spent her life selflessly caring for others instead of worrying about her own schedule. With a heart for music and play, she shares her faith in language that is kid-friendly and emotive. The important thing here is to be authentic—the person you are sharing with wants to hear from you, not from some other speaker or writer you are trying to sound like.

- You could just follow the format of the Apostles' Creed and add some notes or comments about which parts have had special significance in your faith journey. For example, you might say that the forgiveness of sins has always touched your heart, since you had tremendous guilt and despaired of ever finding forgiveness. Or perhaps the fact that the Father created both the heaven and the earth has always mattered to you, since you struggled with atheism or despair that the universe was meaningless.

- Keep this short. It's not a theology textbook, and your reader doesn't want a lecture. The purpose is to clearly and cogently explain what you believe and why it matters so much to you that you've placed your hope in it and built your life around it.

WHO?
YOUR SPECIAL PERSON

DAY 22 • SUNDAY

THEME: Lost and Found

FOCUS: Worship. Rest and trust in the Lord.

Luke 15:1–32

> Now the tax collectors and sinners were all gathering around to hear Jesus. But the Pharisees and the teachers of the law muttered, "This man welcomes sinners and eats with them." Then Jesus told them this parable: "Suppose one of you has a hundred sheep and loses one of them . . .
>
> "Or suppose a woman has ten silver coins and loses one." . . .
> Jesus continued: "There was a man who had two sons. . . ."

Devotional Thoughts

As you begin this last week in our devotional journey and move toward pulling all the pieces together in writing your story, begin by reflecting on how God feels about His lost children. If the person with whom you are planning to share truly matters to you, be assured they matter to God also, far more than you can imagine.

To illustrate this, read Luke 15:1–32. It's the longest passage we'll look at in this devotional journey, an entire chapter, but that's because of the startling point of the three connected parables and the context in which Jesus tells them.

Jesus's enemies are scandalized that He is spending time engaging with those who are far from God. Those who collected taxes for the Roman government had betrayed their Jewish identity and faith. Sinners were people who didn't try hard enough to live by the moral and religious demands of the Jewish faith.

Jesus responds by telling them one story in three parts, and these parts have a unique structure and progression. In all three parts, something important gets lost. The person who loses it expends every effort to find the lost thing. And when the lost thing is found, those around the owner rejoice at its return.

But there's a progression. In the first story, a man loses one sheep from his flock of one hundred—that's one percent of his sheep. Yet he stops at nothing to find it, and there's great rejoicing at the restoration of one percent of his wealth. In the second story, a woman loses one coin out of her ten—which is ten percent of her wealth. Again, she goes to every length to get it back, and there's great rejoicing that ten percent of her wealth is returned.

Then there is a man who loses one of his two sons—fifty percent of his wealth (for children are the greatest wealth God can bless us with). But he doesn't chase the son down, he waits and prays expectantly for his return. When the son comes to his senses, the father spares no dignity or expense in welcoming him back and celebrating his return. Everyone in his household rejoices, except for the other son who is resentful of the father's care and concern for the wandering brother.

Jesus's point is that God's children are worth far more than sheep, coins, or anything else. He waits expectantly to welcome and celebrate their return, and if someone can't understand that then they don't have the Father's heart.

As you prepare to share with someone who may have wandered far from God, remember how valuable they are to the Lord, and how He waits expectantly to welcome their return and how the heavenly host will celebrate.

Worship, rejoice, rest, and know that God knows how much this person matters to you, because they matter even more to Him.

> *Lord, may I never devalue any human being created in your image. They are all your children, though some are lost like the sheep, the coin, or the sons in your parables. May I always assist you in faithfully searching and expectantly waiting for their return and restoration to your household. May I rejoice like the angels in heaven when they are found, just as heaven rejoiced when you found me. Amen.*

ACTIVITY: Worship

We're beginning the last lap of our devotional journey. This week, you'll pull it all together and compose your story, to share the reasons for the hope that you have in Christ, with gentleness and respect. So start the week off the right way: by grounding yourself in worship. Ultimately, that's what all of this is about: not winning an argument or giving the reasons why you believe in a creed. It's about sharing why you trust Jesus, in the prayerful hope that your life and message would be such a testimony to His kingdom that someone else would come to know and love Jesus as well. Today, rest in Christ's love and power, and let His spirit shape your character and words as you reflect and write this week.

WHO?
YOUR SPECIAL PERSON

DAY 23 • MONDAY

THEME: Never Stop Praying

FOCUS: Reflect. Consider the person or persons with whom you want to share.

Colossians 1:9–14

For this reason, since the day we heard about you, we have not stopped praying for you. We continually ask God to fill you with the knowledge of his will through all the wisdom and understanding that the Spirit gives, so that you may live a life worthy of the Lord and please him in every way: bearing fruit in every good work, growing in the knowledge of God, being strengthened with all power according to his glorious might so that you may have great endurance and patience, and giving joyful thanks to the Father, who has qualified you to share in the inheritance of his holy people in the kingdom of light. For he has rescued us from the dominion of darkness and brought us into the kingdom of the Son he loves, in whom we have redemption, the forgiveness of sins.

Devotional Thoughts

You're getting close to putting together the content that will share your faith. You've put a lot of time and effort into this, but you're not done yet.

Nevertheless, if these people are important enough for you to put this much effort into the process of sharing, it would also be wise to pray for them.

As we've seen repeatedly this month, faith is ultimately a gift of the Holy Spirit. He moves and guides our hearts. We can share all knowledge and do enormous amounts of good for others, but without the movement of the Spirit in their lives and hearts they will not be redeemed and transformed by Christ.

As we saw last week, Christ calls us to make disciples by being disciples, to witness to the power of Christ by demonstrating that power in our own hearts and translating it to action in our own lives. God makes spiritual growth in His children the vehicle by which more people are brought to life in Jesus.

> *Lord, forgive me for the times when I failed to pray. Especially forgive me when I failed to pray for someone that you loved and that I wanted to find faith. I don't know why I failed to pray for them, but perhaps I didn't really believe that it would make a difference. Teach me the difference that prayer can make in me, and in others. Amen.*

ACTIVITY: Reflect

Today, reflect on the persons with whom you want to share your faith. The last three weeks you have focused on your story, your reasons for believing, and the substance of your faith. You've worked hard to be prepared to give an answer to someone who asks the reasons for the hope that you have. But remember, Peter tells us that we must share those reasons with gentleness and respect. That's why this week you're not preparing a speech or an essay, but something composed for a specific person or persons. That means bearing in mind who they are and customizing your message— not to change the truth or substance, but to tailor your presentation to their individual needs. Who are they? What drives their life? What are their hopes and fears, strengths and weaknesses?

What is your relationship with them? Pray for insight and clarity, because you want to be insightful and sensitive. As you reflect on this person or persons, jot down some simple notes in your journal. They'll be helpful for your exercises this week.

WHO?
YOUR SPECIAL PERSON

DAY 24 • TUESDAY

THEME: How Much?

FOCUS: Record. List what is best about this person.

John 3:16–17

> For God so loved the world that he gave his one and only Son, that whoever believes in him shall not perish but have eternal life. For God did not send his Son into the world to condemn the world, but to save the world through him.

Devotional Thoughts

As you get closer to writing your story and sharing your faith, it's easy to lose confidence. What if you're ignored or rejected? Maybe it's best to let things be, hope and pray that somehow, someday, they will come around on their own without you having to meddle and risk breaking the relationship.

Truthfully, there is no guarantee that you won't be ignored. Remember, the crowds ultimately rejected Jesus. In fact, the Bible is the story of how mankind continually rejected God, despite all His efforts to be in vital, life-giving relationship with them. From Adam and Eve through the kings and people of Israel, down to the crowds shouting, "Barabbas! Release Barabbas!" God has been patient and longsuffering with a world that causes Him to hurt. And if they treat God that way, how will you be treated?

No matter the response of those around you, the point is that being a disciple of Jesus, a citizen of the kingdom, a believer modeling his or her life on the Master, means having the heart and character of God.

Today, we look at a famous passage that not only summarizes the gospel but gives us real insight into God's own heart. God so loved the world that He gave His only son, not to condemn but to save. If God so loved the world that way, despite its rejection of Him, how can we who follow Him not do the same?

Remember, we are held responsible for our actions, not other people's reactions. Speak with kindness, gentleness, self-control, and above all love. Let your motives and words be God's, and then let the Holy Spirit take it from there.

> *Lord, I confess that I'm afraid of rejection. If I open my heart, tell my story, and share my faith, I am exposed. But you did not hesitate to come and open your heart to me because you loved me. Give me the conviction and courage of your love to speak the truth in love. Amen.*

ACTIVITY: Record

Based on your reflections yesterday, note what is best about the person, or persons, with whom you plan to share your faith. What are their most positive qualities? What's most admirable about them? Because they are made in God's image, even people who struggle with great sin in their lives have the image of God in them.

Your prayer is that the Holy Spirit will use you to speak to that image of God. So, instead of starting with what's worst about this person, begin with what's best. Dwell on that and orient your presentation around appealing to the good within them.

To be clear, on their journey with Christ they will need to deal with the sin in their lives—just as we are still doing, just as you are still doing. And some of that sin might be a river they need to cross to get onto the straight path. But that's not your job. This journey is not about you "fixing" anyone. It's not about telling them what's wrong with their reasons and how they need to change. It's about you sharing the reasons for your hope with gentleness and respect, and praying that you capture their curiosity and touch their heart. In God's time they will have to cross the hard places in their life. But this devotional month isn't about starting in those places.

Don't worry about writing a composed essay. For today, just make some notes, even bullet-style, that will help you frame your approach.

WHO?
YOUR SPECIAL PERSON

DAY 25 • WEDNESDAY

THEME: Each Heart

FOCUS: Record. List what you know of their dreams and struggles.

Proverbs 14:10

Each heart knows its own bitterness, and no one else can share its joy.

Devotional Thoughts

You've been preparing to share your faith with someone who needs it. The question is, why don't they have it now? Why are they far from God? Why don't they hope and believe?

They may have given you reasons. They may have told you that they don't believe because Christians are hypocrites, or don't care enough about the poor or the environment. They may reject Christian sexual morality. They may have told you that God is a fairy tale and they believe in science. They may have been told by professors or even church leaders that the Bible is unreliable, Jesus never rose from the dead or claimed to be God, or that other religions are more authentic.

Remember, those are the reasons they are giving you. They may be true, or they may be intellectual justifications for rejecting God because their heart has been broken.

Many of us have been deeply hurt, even wounded to the core of our being, by life. Maybe it's things that were done to us, or hopes and dreams that never came true. Some of us prayed and never got what we asked for. Some of us feel betrayed. Some of us don't even understand the nature of our pain and disappointments and bitterness, but we have a hard time hearing stories about a loving and caring Father who wants the best for us. Where has He been when we really needed Him?

No one can know the pain of another person's heart. That's why you want to share your reasons for the hope within you instead of arguing with them about the hope you think they should have. Instead of telling them what's wrong with their view of the world, show what's right about yours.

> *Lord, I confess that sometimes I have not been compassionate or sensitive enough toward others who don't believe or follow you. Far too often, I have imagined that their reasons for rejecting you were simple and unworthy. I have not always considered the hurts and fears that might contribute to their actions. As I prepare to share my faith, give me insight into their heart and compassion for their fears. Amen.*

ACTIVITY: Record

Based on your reflections Monday, note what you know about this person's dreams and struggles. What have they hoped for in their life? What have been their disappointments? What pain have they experienced that shaped their perspective? If they don't have faith in Christ, what might be some reasons why they have turned their back on Him, or never even found Him in the first place?

It's easy to say what someone else should do, or should have done. Objectively, there is right and wrong, and people should do the former and avoid the latter. But life is seldom that simple. There are often reasons why someone has made wrong choices. From your perspective, those might be insufficient. Your life experiences and choices led you to faith, theirs did not. I'm not saying that faith or truth is relative. It's not about making excuses, but is about looking for explanations. Unless we have an accurate diagnosis and a good understanding of the problem, we don't know how to present the solutions in a gentle, respectful, and helpful way.

Don't worry about writing a composed essay. For today, just make some notes, even bullet-style, that will help you frame your approach.

WHO?
YOUR SPECIAL PERSON

DAY 26 • THURSDAY

THEME: Dangerous Territory

FOCUS: Record. List the ways that Satan has
lied to them.

1 Peter 5:8–9

Be alert and of sober mind. Your enemy the devil prowls around like a roaring lion looking for someone to devour. Resist him, standing firm in the faith, because you know that the family of believers throughout the world is undergoing the same kind of sufferings.

John 8:44–45

You belong to your father, the devil, and you want to carry out your father's desires. He was a murderer from the beginning, not holding to the truth, for there is no truth in him. When he lies, he speaks his native language, for he is a liar and the father of lies. Yet because I tell the truth, you do not believe me!

2 Corinthians 11:14

And no wonder, for Satan himself masquerades as an angel of light.

Devotional Thoughts

As you share your faith, you're entering dangerous territory. We cannot read the Bible honestly and deny the reality of Satan, a spiritual enemy who opposes God and His people.

Satan lies to keep us from God. That's how he led Adam and Eve into their fall. He has blinded and deceived his way through the ages. He even appears good and beautiful when it suits his purposes, but it's all a fraud. His goal is to cheat and steal, to rob us of eternal life and give us nothing in return.

Do not underestimate him. He is a creature of immense intelligence and power. He will not easily give up. He will do what he has always done: twist words, mixing just enough truth into his lies to make them seem plausible, but always keeping those who he has blinded from seeing clearly.

Because if they did, they would all reject his empty show.

As you share your faith, keep it simple. The correct response from Adam and Eve, when asked whether God had really said they shall not eat from the tree of the Knowledge of Good and Evil, should have been, "Yes, he really did say that."

Complex arguments about theological nuances aren't helpful at this point. The simple truth is the best. And although we start simple, our faith is not simplistic. The one thing that Satan cannot stand against is the simple truth that Jesus came in the flesh, that He is Lord, and that we trust His Word. Start there, and don't let the enemy make it all into a muddle.

> *Lord, protect me from my spiritual enemy. I know that he seeks to deceive and destroy, but I know that you are far stronger, and he cannot stand against your name and power. By your Holy Spirit, let me see through the enemy's lies, and may your Spirit protect the person I am writing to and sharing with, that they would see and know the truth. Amen.*

ACTIVITY: Record

Based on your reflections Monday, note what you know about the ways Satan has lied to this person, and what truths will set them free of those lies. As we saw in our devotion today, Satan is a liar. Jesus calls him the father of lies. The Bible tells us that he can appear as an angel of light when he chooses, luring people with promised wisdom and power. That's how he persuaded Adam and Eve to disobey God, bringing sin into the world. Ever since then, we've all been subject to his flattering, his deception, his twisting of words, and his empty promises.

The people with whom you wish to share the gospel have heard Satan's lies (we all have) and they have warped their view of life and God (just as our views are sometimes warped). The difference is that you now have the presence of the Holy Spirit in your life through Christ, countering Satan's seducing whispers. The person, or persons, that you have in mind are without God's active presence in their life, shepherding them through this dark world.

Note what you know about what false ideas and ideologies they labor under. Note what lies they believe about themselves, about you, and about God. To effectively present your reasons with gentleness and respect, you have to take these into account because the Enemy wants to turn them away from the gospel. So it's important that you choose your words and direct your remarks to have as much influence as possible. With the help of the Holy Spirit, work to win them back.

Don't worry about writing a composed essay. For today, just make some notes, even bullet-style, that will help you frame your approach.

WHO?
YOUR SPECIAL PERSON

DAY 27 • FRIDAY

THEME: How Can They

FOCUS: Read. Review the notes you made this week.

Romans 10:9–17

If you declare with your mouth, "Jesus is Lord," and believe in your heart that God raised him from the dead, you will be saved. For it is with your heart that you believe and are justified, and it is with your mouth that you profess your faith and are saved. As Scripture says, "Anyone who believes in him will never be put to shame." For there is no difference between Jew and Gentile—the same Lord is Lord of all and richly blesses all who call on him, for, "Everyone who calls on the name of the Lord will be saved."

How, then, can they call on the one they have not believed in? And how can they believe in the one of whom they have not heard? And how can they hear without someone preaching to them? And how can anyone preach unless they are sent? As it is written: "How beautiful are the feet of those who bring good news!"

But not all the Israelites accepted the good news. For Isaiah says, "Lord, who has believed our message?" Consequently, faith comes from hearing the message, and the message is heard through the word about Christ.

Devotional Thoughts

By and large, God does the work of the gospel through His people. We are the body of Christ in this world.

It's easy to be overwhelmed by the needs of the world. But you aren't responsible for fixing the world. We are responsible for being witnesses to the power of the resurrection and for representing Christ where we are and to those God has put before us. Sometimes we are supposed to be the mouth of Christ, when we share His message.

In our Scripture today, Paul tells us that, "Faith comes from hearing the message, and the message is heard through the word about Christ" (Romans 10:17). You are preparing to share with someone who needs to hear, which means that someone needs to tell them "the word about Christ." Will you do it with great eloquence and sophistication? Probably not. But do you know what you can bring to your presentation? Love and sincerity. If you could persuade the world's most eloquent, educated, and sophisticated Christian writer, speaker, and evangelist to come and make the presentation on your behalf, it might be more polished and sophisticated. But that person couldn't be more loving and sincere than you. You can bring that to the table.

Accept that role. Near the beginning of his prophecy, Isaiah describes how he got his job. He was given a vision of the throne room of God, which just made him realize how inadequate he was. But God asks all the angelic host assembled there who would go and bring His message to the Israelites. Isaiah is undone, because he knows that despite his inadequacy, it is his responsibility. He calls out, "Here am I. Send me" (Isaiah 6:8).

You care about someone, and you want him or her to come to faith. Someone should do something about that, right?

Lord, I am not worthy to be your witness. You have so many followers that are smarter, better educated, and more effective communicators. But if you are calling me to be the one to deliver your message, may I be full of love for you and them, and sincere in my desire to speak the truth in that love. Amen.

ACTIVITY: Read

Today, read what you wrote in your journal and other notes this week. Reflect and pray over what you've recorded. Is it accurate? What did you learn? What insights did you capture? What surprised you? How do you feel about it?

What's most important? What's wonderful? Did you leave anything out, get anything wrong, or misrepresent the truth in any way? Organize your thoughts, make additions, corrections and tweaks, because tomorrow you'll take a retreat to pull the last month together and compose your story.

WHO?
YOUR SPECIAL PERSON

DAY 28 • SATURDAY

THEME: Put It All Together

FOCUS: Retreat and write. Pull it all together and compose your story.

1 Peter 3:15–16

> But in your hearts revere Christ as Lord. Always be prepared to give an answer to everyone who asks you to give the reason for the hope that you have. But do this with gentleness and respect, keeping a clear conscience, so that those who speak maliciously against your good behavior in Christ may be ashamed of their slander.

Devotional Thoughts

This is a big day! For twenty-seven days you've worshiped, prayed, reflected, studied, and jotted down notes. Today, you take a retreat and pull it all together. Today, you're going to go back over all the notes you've compiled and compose your complete story—a letter to the special person with whom you want to share your faith.

We know it's a little overwhelming. That's why today we want you to come back to where you began. Read today's Scripture. It's the passage upon which this whole devotional project is based. What does it say?

"Do not fear their threats; do not be frightened" (1 Peter 3:14). The person with whom you share probably won't threaten you, but you're probably frightened that they might be offended and it could start an argument. The beginning of that verse reads, "But even if you should suffer for what is right, you are blessed." Doing the right thing for the right reasons pleases God.

Peter grounds us in the foundation of all spiritual service: "In your hearts revere Christ as Lord." That's why you've spent a month worshiping, praying, and reflecting on the Scriptures before writing your faith story. Your witness has to be authentic, built on the foundation of worship and reverence for Christ. If it isn't, the person you share with will see right through it.

And Peter comes to the purpose of this whole project: "Always be prepared to give an answer to everyone who asks you to give the reason for the hope that you have. But do this with gentleness and respect, keeping a clear conscience, so that those who speak maliciously against your good behavior in Christ may be ashamed of their slander" (1 Peter 3:15–16).

Keep in mind the purpose of this devotional journey and the content you're compiling. You're not here to defeat their arguments or analyze their resistance to the gospel to show them how inadequate their reasons are for hanging or pushing back. Your purpose is not to convert them. In fact, you're not even trying to persuade them.

You're sharing the reasons for your hope and faith in Christ, with gentleness and respect. Do that, and let the Holy Spirit make the next move. Follow where He leads.

Lord, thank you for leading me through this journey for the last month. Now, as I prepare to share the reasons for my hope, may you give clarity to my mind, joy to my heart, power to my words, and gentleness and respect to my tone and demeanor. May it not be me that they hear, Lord, but you speaking through me. Amen.

ACTIVITY: Retreat and Write

Today, you're going to take the final writing retreat of this devotional month, and this one isn't so mini. You're going need time to pull all the pieces you've composed over the last month together and compose a summary presentation. It will take a bit more time than the last three retreats. So, what has worked for you? Draw on those experiences to organize a bit more time today. With God's help, figure it out and do your best.

Go over the letters or essays you composed on your last three retreats. Those would be your faith story, the list of reasons for your faith, and your faith statement. Also, review the notes you pulled together yesterday about the specific person or persons for whom you want to compose this summary. With all of that in hand and in mind, bring them together into one document.

There are several ways that you could do this. You could compose an introduction and conclusion, and sandwich the three documents between them. If they are well-written and compelling and you think that stylistically it would work for the person, then do that. Or you might want to weave them together into an integrated presentation of your life, how and why you became a follower of Christ, what you believe and why those beliefs are so important to you. You might include photos or images that help tell the story and would help someone understand you and what matters to you.

Week Four Retreat
Tips for Sharing Your Reasons for Faith

- Reread 1 Peter 3:15–16. That's the Bible passage that has framed this whole project. Before you prepare to share, ground yourself by reexamining it: "But in your hearts revere Christ as Lord. Always be prepared to give an answer to everyone who asks you to give the reason for the hope that you have. But do this with gentleness and respect, keeping a clear conscience, so that those who speak maliciously against your good behavior in Christ may be ashamed of their slander."

- Examine your conscience. Reflect on your motives for sharing, on your own relationship with Christ, and how you actually live out your own faith. In your heart, do you revere Christ as Lord? It isn't fair to ask others to do so if you don't yourself. We don't measure ourselves against other people, we measure ourselves against Christ. And that ought to make us humble and kind. After all, in the Lord's prayer we ask to be forgiven as we forgive those who have sinned against us. So, as you prepare to share your faith, check your heart to be sure that your spirit is being led by the Holy Spirit.

- Examine your demeanor. Most of our interpersonal communication is nonverbal. Which means that your facial expressions, body language, and tone of voice convey more substance than your words. You can say that you're sharing out of love, but if your demeanor is not loving, then they won't hear you, or even worse will accuse you of hypocrisy. Does your demeanor convey gentleness and respect? As Peter says, if it does, then it will be difficult for someone (perhaps the person you share with) to speak maliciously against you. If your demeanor doesn't convey gentleness and respect, then you've given them grounds to reject and criticize your attempts to share your hope in Christ.

- Examine your expectations. What you're hoping for is that the person with whom you share responds by accepting Christ, or returning to the faith. That's the ultimate goal, but it may not happen immediately. Think about your own faith journey. What you share with them might be a stepping stone on that journey, or a chapter in their eventual faith story, but it could take years (or decades) for that to bear fruit. Make it your primary goal to be genuinely heard, then let the Holy Spirit make the next move in His own time.

- Make sure you frame this as being about your own journey. You're sharing *your* story, *your* reasons for hope. The point isn't to talk about their story, or their reasons for not hoping. Share your faith, then pray that those ideas will connect with them.

- Pray! You need the Holy Spirit to prepare the hearts, words, attitudes, and demeanors of both you and the person with whom you will share. Prepare with faithful, sincere, consistent prayer as you write your story. Ask others to pray with and for you.

- Carefully consider how to follow up. Neither of us knows how your story will be received, so we can't tell you how to follow up before it happens. But there are two considerations you should keep in mind. First, if you are sincere in your love for this person, then you don't drop a sermon or book on them and abandon the relationship. If you genuinely care, then your caring relationship should be a constant, whether they respond positively or not. So share your faith in the context of a consistent, loving relationship, and patiently pray for it to bear fruit according to God's will and timing.

AFTERWORD

So here is the rest of the story that began in the introduction . . . After seven years of our lives intersecting over the topic of faith, I felt it was time to give my son the written story of my life in Christ.

Here is his response:

> When my dad first handed his story to me, I wept as I realized that he had poured his heart and soul into sharing his story with me. It meant so much that he would share his journey with me as I am on my own journey to a relationship with God. The book was amazing, made me tear up a few times every time I read it. . . . This book is something I will keep with me forever. It's a resource that I will be able to use for the rest of my life during the hard times and the good. . . . I will be able to share this with my future wife and kids.

So what's your next step?

- Compose a letter that includes your faith story for one of the people on your list?
- Record your story on video for your grandchild who lives out of state?

- Practice verbally sharing your story and schedule a lunch with one of the people God has laid on your heart?
- Create a memory book that includes pictures and contains the story of your life in Christ?
- Do more research on why Christianity is true?

There is no one right answer, but we all are called to give a reason for the Hope that lies within us.

If you would like resources and support for writing your story, researching Christianity, or learning about the many ways you can share your story, please visit our website, www.MH2U.org.

Everyone has a story, let us help you tell yours.

—Merlin and Theresa Buhl

Theresa and Merlin Buhl are cofounders of My Hope to You, a ministry dedicated to helping Christians share what they believe and why in the context of their own story.

Theresa is a graduate of Hope College where she received a degree in special education—a degree well-used as she homeschooled their children. Theresa has a passion for prayer and helping people get set free from what enslaves them. Merlin graduated from Hope College and Trinity Evangelical Divinity School with a master's degree in counseling psychology. Studying under Dr. William Lane Craig at TEDS ignited his passion for making Christian apologetics understandable and relatable to real life.

They both believe that sharing the reasons for the hope that lies within us is the best way to organically share Jesus with others. Happily married for over thirty years, they reside in Holland, Michigan, and have just recently become empty nesters after raising nine children, four cats, and a dog.

NAME _____ PHONE (H) _____

ADDRESS _____ PHONE (W) _____

_____ FAX _____

EMAIL _____ CELL/PAGER _____

NAME _____ PHONE (H) _____

ADDRESS _____ PHONE (W) _____

_____ FAX _____

EMAIL _____ CELL/PAGER _____

NAME _____ PHONE (H) _____

ADDRESS _____ PHONE (W) _____

_____ FAX _____

EMAIL _____ CELL/PAGER _____

NAME _____ PHONE (H) _____

ADDRESS _____ PHONE (W) _____

_____ FAX _____

EMAIL _____ CELL/PAGER _____

NAME _____ PHONE (H) _____

ADDRESS _____ PHONE (W) _____

_____ FAX _____

EMAIL _____ CELL/PAGER _____

NAME _____ PHONE (H) _____

ADDRESS _____ PHONE (W) _____

_____ FAX _____

EMAIL _____ CELL/PAGER _____

NAME

ADDRESS

EMAIL

PHONE (H)

PHONE (W)

FAX

CELL/PAGER

NAME

ADDRESS

EMAIL

PHONE (H)

PHONE (W)

FAX

CELL/PAGER

NAME

ADDRESS

EMAIL

PHONE (H)

PHONE (W)

FAX

CELL/PAGER

NAME

ADDRESS

EMAIL

PHONE (H)

PHONE (W)

FAX

CELL/PAGER

NAME

ADDRESS

EMAIL

PHONE (H)

PHONE (W)

FAX

CELL/PAGER

NAME

ADDRESS

EMAIL

PHONE (H)

PHONE (W)

FAX

CELL/PAGER

NAME

ADDRESS

EMAIL

PHONE (H)

PHONE (W)

FAX

CELL/PAGER

NAME

ADDRESS

EMAIL

PHONE (H)

PHONE (W)

FAX

CELL/PAGER

NAME

ADDRESS

EMAIL

PHONE (H)

PHONE (W)

FAX

CELL/PAGER

NAME

ADDRESS

EMAIL

PHONE (H)

PHONE (W)

FAX

CELL/PAGER

NAME

ADDRESS

EMAIL

PHONE (H)

PHONE (W)

FAX

CELL/PAGER

NAME

ADDRESS

EMAIL

PHONE (H)

PHONE (W)

FAX

CELL/PAGER

NAME

ADDRESS

EMAIL

PHONE (H)

PHONE (W)

FAX

CELL/PAGER

NAME

ADDRESS

EMAIL

PHONE (H)

PHONE (W)

FAX

CELL/PAGER

NAME

ADDRESS

EMAIL

PHONE (H)

PHONE (W)

FAX

CELL/PAGER

NAME

ADDRESS

EMAIL

PHONE (H)

PHONE (W)

FAX

CELL/PAGER

NAME

ADDRESS

EMAIL

PHONE (H)

PHONE (W)

FAX

CELL/PAGER

NAME

ADDRESS

EMAIL

PHONE (H)

PHONE (W)

FAX

CELL/PAGER